Pascal Programming:

230⁺ Questions And Answers

Hensley Pink

Pascal Programming: 230⁺ Questions and Answers

Published by: Hensley Pink

Printed in the United States of America

ISBN: 9781983107375

Acknowledgements

My unfathomable gratitude to the Almighty God for empowering, inspiring creative thinking that is prompted.

Special thanks to Mr. Frantz-Earl Robinson (poet, author and guitarist) who persistently encouraged me to become an Amazon author and publisher. Thanks, also, to the many persons who expressed commendations for a lot of my literary creations. They repeatedly stated commend my efforts and constantly wish me success in such pursuits.

Special acknowledgement to my 2 lovely daughters, **Andrene** and **Andrea**. I love them a whole lot and they are my special, adoring fans. They pray and hope that all my pursuits end successfully. They are specially fascinated and thrilled over my creative expressions and no doubt will greatly relish this publication. They continue to inspire an abundance of courage and confidence. I duly recognize them for contributing greatly, though indirectly, to the publishing of this proposal.

PREFACE

This book is intended for high school students who do Programming in Pascal. It functions as a supplement to general Pascal texts. The questions are categorized according to the syllabus that is used by Caribbean students but may be generally used for 4th and 5th form English-speaking students living anywhere in the world. It is useful to beginners and intermediate adult students of Pascal.

BASIC FORMAT OF A PASCAL PROGRAM

1. **Which of the following is <u>NOT</u> a Pascal keyword?**

   a. Program

   b. Programs

   c. Program

   d. PROGRAM

2. **Which of the following is a Pascal identifier?**

   a. Program

   b. End

   c. Begin

   d. TITLE

3. **Which of the following is <u>NOT</u> an identifier?**

   a. Title

   b. End

   c. Age

   d. Num

4. **Which statement is correct?**

   a. Programs Math;

   b. Program Math:

   c. Program math,

   d. PROGRAM math;

5. **Which of the following statement is <u>NOT</u> true?**

    a. The number of statements between 'Begin and 'End' is finite.

    b. The number of statements between 'Begin' and 'End' is infinite.

    c. An identifier may be made up of digits, hyphens and other characters.

    d. A Pascal statement without a semicolon (;) at the end may be correct.

USING THE WRITE STATEMENT

6. **Which statement is true?**

    a. The **Write** statement is <u>NOT</u> associated with output from the computer.

    b. The **write** statement is associated with output from the computer.

    c. The purpose of the **write** statement is to accept input from the keyboard.

    d. The **write** statement is used to store data.

7. **Which statement is <u>NOT</u> true?**

    a. Every **write** statement may have a full stop at the end.

    b. **Write** statements are always associated with output.

    c. **Write** statements may have a semi-colon at the end.

    d. A **write** statement may be used to print text on the monitor.

8. **Which statement is true?**

    a. Double quotes must be used to enclose messages in the **write** statement.

    b. Single quotes used with the **write** statements do not have to be used in pairs.

    c. No more than 2 quotes may be used with one **write** statement.

    d.   Double quotes may be used within single quotes with the **write** statement.

9. **Which write statement is correct?**

   a. **Write**('Hello);

   b. **Write**('Hello'),

   c. **Write**('Hello');

   d. **Write**("hello");

10. **Which write statement is <u>NOT</u> correct?**

    a. **Write** ('Hello, I'am ok.');

    b. **Write**('Hello, I''ll return');

    c. **Write** ('Hello, I am here.');

    d. **Write**('hello, I am ok');

USING THE WRITELN STATEMENT

11. **Which statement is true?**

    a. The **writeln** statement is <u>NOT</u> associated with output from the computer.

    b. The **writeln** statement is associated with output from the computer.

    c. The purpose of the **writeln** statement is to accept input from the keyboard.

    d. The **writeln** statement is used to store data.

12. **Which statement is <u>NOT</u> true?**

    a. Every **writeln** statement may have a semi-colon at the end.

    b. **Writeln** statements function exactly as **write** statements.

    c. **Writeln** statements are useful in generating blank lines in the output.

    d. A **writeln** statement may not output a message.

13. Which statement is true?

    a.   Double quotes must be used to enclose messages in the **writeln** statement.

    b.   Single quotes used with the **writeln** statements do not have to be used in pairs.

    c.   No more than 2 quotes may be used with one **writeln** statement.

    d.   Double quotes may be used with the **writeln** statement.

14. Which writeln statement is correct?

    a.   Writeln (").

    b.   Writeln('Hello'),

    c.   Writeln('Hello');

    d.   Writeln("hello");

15. Which writeln statement is NOT correct?

    a.   **Write**ln ('Hello, I'am ok.');

    b.   **Write**ln('Hello, I''ll return');

    c.   **Write**ln ('Hello, I am here.');

    d.   **Write**ln('hello, I am ok');

16. What is the main difference between write and writeln?

    a.   The **writeln** statement leaves the cursor in the middle of the next line, rather than at the end of the current line.

    b.   The **writeln** statement leaves the cursor at the beginning of the current output line, rather than than at the end of the current line.

    c.   The **write** statement leaves the cursor at the beginning of the next line, rather than at the end of the current line.

    d.   The **write** statement leaves the cursor either at the beginning of the next line or at the end of the current line.

17. Which of the program segments would give the following output?

Welcome

to

Pascal

a. *Begin*

    Writeln ('Welcome ');

    Write ('to ');

    Writeln ('Pascal.')

  end.

b. *Begin*

    Writeln ('Welcome ');

    Writeln ('to ');

    Writeln ('Pascal.')

  end.

c. *Begin*

    Write ('Welcome ');

    Writeln ('to ');

    Writeln ('Pascal.')

  end.

d. *Begin*

    Write ('Welcome ');

    Write ('to ');

    Writeln ('Pascal.')

  end.

STANDARD DATA TYPES

18. Which value is an integer?

    a. -327800

    b. 327800

    c. 30000

    d. 3278000

19. Which value is <u>NOT</u> an integer?

    a. -427

    b. -1000

    c. 0

    d. -32769

20. The range, IE-28 – IE+38, represents --------------- values.

    a. Integer

    b. Real

    c. Character

    d. Boolean

21. The values, 0.0 and 3.8, are -------------- values.

    a. Boolean

    b. Character

    c. Integer

    d. Real

22. How many Boolean values exist?

    a. 2

    b. 4

    c. 6

    d. 8

23. TRUE and FALSE are -------------- values.

    a. Boolean

    b. Char

    c. Integer

    d. Real

24. Which is a char value?

    a. a

    b. 'joy'

    c. 'h'

    d. 3

25. Div and mod are permissible operations for ----------- values.

    a. Real

    b. Integer

    c. Char

    d. Boolean

26. To which set may addition, subtraction and multiplication be applied?

a. Char and integer

b. Integer and Boolean

c. Real and integer

d. Boolean and char

27. To which data type does negation apply?

a. Integer

b. Boolean

c. Char

d. Real

28. To which data type does concatenation apply?

a. Integer

b. Char

c. Boolean

d. Real

29. Any one element of the ASCII set is a/an ------------- value.

a. Char

b. Integer

c. Real

d. Boolean

30. Which operation is <u>NOT</u> permissible?

    a. 12.8 + 2

    b. 4.0 * 1.2

    c. 10 mod 2

    d. 10/2

31. Which operation is permissible?

    a. 'a' * 2

    b. a mod b

    c. 12.7 div 3

    d. 0.4 mod 0.2

32. Which data type permits the narrowest range of operations?

    a. Integer

    b. Real

    c. Char

    d. Boolean

GUIDELINES FOR NAMING VARIABLES

33. Which character must <u>NOT</u> be used to begin a variable name?

    a. !

    b. t

    c. H

    d. Z

34. **Which character may be used to begin a variable name?**

    a. *

    b. –

    c. Y

    d. &

35. Which is <u>NOT</u> a valid variable?

    a. Name

    b. _Age

    c. DOB

    d. D65

36. Which is a valid variable?

    a. *hut1

    b. =total

    c. !address

    d. School

37. A Pascal variable name may have up to ----------- characters.

    a. 32

    b. 30

    c. 28

    d. 20

38. The 1st ------- characters of a variable name are unique.

    a. 14

    b. 12

    c. 10

    d. 8

39. Which statement about variable names is true?

    a. They are not case sensitive.

    b. They are case sensitive.

    c. They must always begin with uppercase characters.

    d. They may not contain blank characters.

40. Meaningful variable names help in creating --------- programs.

    a. shorter

    b. correct

    c. readable

    d. longer

41. Which variable is most meaningful for a student's file?

    a. Sc

    b. Sch

    c. Schl

    d. School

42. Which is the least meaningful variable for a payroll file?

   a. Net Pay

   b. N_Pay

   c. N_P

   d. Net_P

DECLARING VARIABLES (1)

43. Which statement is true?

   a. Variables may be declared at any point in the program.

   b. Variables must be declared before they are used.

   c. Variables representing integers must be declared before any other.

   d. No more than one variable may be declared in one line.

44. Which statement is TRUE?

   a. The word 'var' must be used before any variable is declared.

   b. The variable type may not be acknowledged in the declaration.

   c. A full stop must be used after every variable that is declared.

   d. A colon is used to separate variables on a line.

45. Which statement is <u>NOT</u> true?

   a. A list of variables may be declared on the same line.

   b. One data type declaration may be applied to a list of variables of the same type.

   c. Variables for different data types may not be declared on the same line.

   d. Boolean variables must be declared after all other variables.

46. Which statement about variables is true?

   a. A real variable cannot accept any integer value .

   b. An integer variable may accept real values in special situations.

   c. A real variable may accept integer values.

   d. A Boolean variable may accept ASCII values.

47. Which variable is most suited to be declared to be used as a flag or switch?

   a. Integer

   b. Real

   c. Char

   d. boolean

DECLARING VARIABLES (2)

48. Which declaration is correct?

   a. Var num1; integer;

   b. Var: num1 integer;

   c. Var num1: integer;

   d. Var num1: integer.

49. Which declaration is <u>NOT</u> correct?

   a. Var m,n,p: real;

   b. Var m;p: integer;

   c. Var m,p: integer;

   d. Var initial: char;

50. How many times is the word 'var' needed if 4 variables are to be declared?

    a. 4

    b. 3

    c. 2

    d. 1

51. Which declaration is correct?

    a. Var x: integer;

            y: real;

    b. Var: Integer, y: real.

    c. Var x   integer.

            y: real;

    d. Var y:real, x:integer;

52. Which declaration is correct if the '6' and '4.5' must be input?

    a. Var m,n: integer;

    b. Var n,m: integer;

    c. Var m: integer;

            n:real;

    d. Var m,n:real;

ASSIGNING DATA TO VARIABLES

53. Which operator is used for assigning data to variables?

    a. +

    b. #

    c. =

    d. :=

54. Which statement is true?

    a. Data may be assigned to variables by using the 'var' statement.

    b. Data may be assigned during variable declaration.

    c. Integer data may be assigned to Integer variables, only.

    d. The assignment operator is used to assign data to any variable.

55. Which assignment statement is correct?

    a. a = 2

    b. a:= 2

    c. a;= 2

    d. a =: 2

56. Which of the following statement is <u>NOT</u> an assignment statement?

    a. a := b + c

    b. a > b + c

    c. b := c − a

    d. a:= b

57. If a =6, which statement will result in y being 12?

a. y = a + a

b. y = 12

c. y:= a

d. y:= a * 2

GETTING DATA INTO VARIABLES USING 'READ/READLN'

58. The purpose of read is to ---------- data.

a. Store

b. Transmit

c. Input

d. Process

59. The purpose of readln is to accept data from ……....

a. Tape

b. File

c. Record

d. The keyboard

60. Which statement is correct?

a. Read(x),

b. Read(x);

c. Read ('x');

d. Read (x).

61. Which statement is <u>NOT</u> correct?

    a. Readln (x,y);

    b. Readln ('y');

    c. Readln(x);

    d. Readln(y);

62. Which statement about read/readln is true?

    a. They sometimes output information.

    b. There is no difference in how they function.

    c. They function after a program is finished executing.

    d. They both facilitate interactive programming.

READ VS READLN

63. Where does the major difference between read and readln lie?

    a. The treatment of string values

    b. The amount of input allowed

    c. The speed of input

    d. The nature of processing

64. Which statement about read and readln is true?

    a. Both are output statements.

    b. There is no difference between them when working with integers.

    c. Read works on integers while readln works with strings.

    d. Both may be used in one instruction.

65. **Two string values must be input on separate lines. Which set would facilitate the input as required?**

   a.   readln (x);   read (x); read (y)

   b.   readln (x); readln(y);

   c.   read(x);   read(y);

   d.   read(y); readln(y); read(x);

66. **Two string values must be input on the same line. Which set is correct?**

   a.   readln(a); read (b);

   b.   read(b); read(a);

   c.   read(a; read (b);

   d.   readln(b); readln(b);

67. **Two integer values must be input on the same line and the cursor must be positioned at the beginning of the next line. Which statement set is correct?**

   a.   Read(n):readln(m);

   b.   read(m); read(n);

   c.   readln(m); read(n);

   d.   read(m); readln(m);

USING VARIABLES IN OUTPUT

68. **If x= 4 and y=2, which statement would output the values as follows: 4 + 2 = 6**

   a.   Write(x + y = x, y);

   b.   Write('x'+ 'y' = 4 + 2);

   c.   Writeln(x, '+' ,y ,'=', x + y);

   d.   Writeln('y'+ 'x' = x + y);

69. If x= 6 and twice the value of x must be output. Which statement is correct?

    a. Write(x,x);

    b. Write('x,x');

    c. Write(x*2);

    d. Write(x*x);

70. Which statement is true?

    a. Values of variables can be output directly

    b. Variables may not be used in arithmetic operations with **'write'**.

    c. Variables must be enclosed in single quotation marks for output.

    d. String variables are not used directly in output statements.

71. If x=2 and y=4, what would be the output from write ('x', 'y')?

    a. 2,4

    b. y,x

    c. xy

    d. 4,2

72. If x=2 and y=4, what would the output from write(x+y, y*x)?

    a. 2,4 4,2

    b. 6,24

    c. 24,6

    d. 4,2 2,4

FORMATTING REAL VARIABLES

73. Which statement is true?

    a.   Real values may be formatted to a specified number of significant digits

    b.   Real values cannot be formatted to a set number of decimal places.

    c.   Real values cannot have more than 5 significant digits.

    d.   In formatting real values, the number of decimal places must be specified first.

74. Which of the following statement is <u>NOT</u> true?

    a.   Real variables with zero values may be formatted to a specified number of significant digits.

    b.   Real variables with negative values are treated like those with positive values.

    c.   Real variables with zero values cannot be formatted.

    d.   A specified number of character spaces must be reserved to accommodate the number of significant digits to be displayed for real variables.

75. Which of the output is formatted to facilitate 3 significant digits?

    a.   Write(x:2:3);

    b.   Write(x:3:2);

    c.   Write(3:2:x);

    d.   Write(2:3:x);

76. Which output is formatted to facilitate 3 decimal places?

    a.   Write(x:2:3);

    b.   Write(x:3:2);

    c.   Write(3:2:x);

    d.   Write(2:3:x);

77. If X is a real variable with a value of 3.5, what is the most likely result to be displayed by the following? Write(x)

a. 3.5

b. 3.50

c. 3.500000E+00

d. 3.5000000000E+00

78. If X is a real variable with a value of 3.5, what is the most likely result to be displayed by the following? Write(x:4:2)

a. 3.5

b. 3.50

c. 3.500000E+00

d. 3.5000000000E+00

MAKING DECISIONS

79. Which statement about making decisions is true?

a. It mainly involves the use of arithmetic operators.

b. It mainly involves the use of logical operators.

c. It mainly involves the use of relational operators in conditions.

d. It must include the use of parentheses in conditions.

80. Which statement is <u>NOT</u> true?

a. Making decision in Pascal is facilitated by 'if-then', only.

b. Making decisions in Pascal is facilitated by 'if-then-else', only.

c. Making decisions in Pascal is facilitated both by 'if-then-else' and 'if-then'.

d. Making decisions in Pascal is not facilitated by 'if-then-else' nor 'if-then'.

81. Which operator indicates that one value is the same as another?

    a. >

    b. <

    c. <>

    d. =

82. Which operator indicates that one value is not the same as another?

    a. >

    b. <

    c. <>

    d. =

83. Which operator indicates that one value is of a higher value than another?

    a. >

    b. >=

    c. <

    d. <=

84. Which operator indicates that one value is of a lower value than another?

    a. >

    b. >=

    c. <

    d. <=

85. Which operator indicates that one value is the same as, or is of a higher value than another?

    a. >

    b. >=

    c. <

    d. <=

86. Which operator indicates that one value is the same as, or is of a lower value than another?

    a. >

    b. >=

    c. <

    d. <=

THE IF-THEN STATEMENT

87. Which statement about the if-then statement is true?

    a. It can contain 1 condition, only.

    b. It must contain at least 2 conditions.

    c. It must have at least 1 condition.

    d. It is not required to have a condition.

88. The if-then statement is expected to return a/an -------------- result.

    a. arithmetic

    b. logical

    c. relational

    d. integer

89. The result from the if-then statement is used to -------------- an action to be taken.

   a. determine

   b. test

   c. Cancel

   d. Preview

90. The if-then statement may contain -------------------.

   a. Any other Pascal statements

   b. An assignment or an output statement, only

   c. An input statement, only

   d. No other statement.

91. The if-then statement can specify up to ---- resulting actions.

   a. 2

   b. 3

   c. 5

   d. 6

92. The if-then statement sometimes combines several ------------- in deciding the resulting action to be taken.

   a. Statements

   b. Operators

   c. Conditions

   d. Operands

93. Every if-then statement must have at least ----- resulting action(s).

a. 1

b. 2

c. 3

d. 4

94. Which statement about resulting actions in the if-then statement is <u>FALSE</u>?

a. They cannot include if-then statements.

b. Then may include input statements

c. They may include any Pascal statement.

d. They may include arithmetic operations.

THE IF-THEN-ELSE STATEMENT

95. Which statement about if-then-else is true?

a. It is an alternative to **if-then**

b. It is an extension of **if-then**

c. It is a replacement of **if-then**

d. It has the same function as **if-then**

96. Which statement about if-then-else is <u>FALSE</u>?

a. It has a wider function than **if-then**.

b. The 'else' means 'otherwise' in everyday language.

c. It must use more than 1 condition.

d. More than 1 resulting action must be specified.

97. If the condition in an if-then-else statement is true, what will follow?

a.   The action(s) specified by **else** will be executed.

b.   The action(s) specified by **then** will be executed.

c.   The action(s) specified by **else** may not be executed.

d.   The actions specified by **then** may be executed.

98. A computer program is to decide if a score is a pass. If it is a pass, then a message must be printed. Which statement is true as it relates to the decision?

a.   An **if-then** statement, only, is needed.

b.   Both an **if-then** and an **if-then-else** statement are needed.

c.   Neither an **if-then** nor an **if-then-else** statement is needed.

d.   The decision cannot be made unless an **if-then-else** statement is used.

99. A score is to be input and classified by grade, A-F. Which statement is true re the classification?

a.   An **if-then** statement may be used.

b.   Both an **if-then** and an **if-then-else** statement are needed.

c.   Neither an **if-then** nor an **if-then-else** statement is needed.

d.   An **if-then-else** statement should be used.

100.   Two values, x and y, are to be input and tested for equality. A message must be output stating 'equal' or 'unequal'. Which statement is correct?

a.   If x = y then write ('equal') or write('unequal');

b.   If x = y then write ('unequal') or write('equal');

c.   If x = y then write ('unequal') else write('equal');

d.   If x = y then write ('equal') else write('unequal');

101. Two values, x and y, are to be input. They must be output if they are not equal. If they are equal, a message, only, is output. Which statement is correct?

    a. If x= y then write ('equal) else write (x,y);

    b. If x > y then write ('unequal) else write(x,y);

    c. If x= y then write('unequal) else write('x,y);

    d. If x= y then write (x) else write (y);

102. If x=2 and y =4, what should be the output from the following?
If x<y then write ('less than') else if y > x write('greater than');

    a. 2

    b. 4

    c. Less than

    d. Greater than

Multi-conditional statements using AND

103. Which statement is true?

    a. A multi-conditional statement is another name for the **if-then-else** statement.

    b. An if-then statement cannot be a multi-conditional statement.

    c. A multi-conditional statement must have a logical operator.

    d. **At** least 3 conditions must be present for a statement to be termed multi-conditional.

104. Which is **NOT** a multi-conditional expression?

    a. If (x < 6)

    b. If (x>4) AND (y<x)

    c. If(b=9) AND (r=t)

    d. If (x) AND (y)

105. A value must be tested to determine if it is an even number. It must also be determined if it is less than 100 so that it may be output. Why is AND needed in the condition?

a. To indicate that the number has 2 values

b. 'AND' must be included in a multi-conditional statement

c. The 2 conditions must be met for output to take place.

d. There are 2 conditions, only.

106. A value must be tested to determine if it is an even number. It must also be determined if it is less than 100 so that it may be output. Which statement is correct?

a. If (x mod 2 = 0) AND (x < 100) then write(x);

b. If (x mod 2 = 0) AND (< 100) then write(x);

c. If (x mod 2 = 0) AND < 100 then write(x);

d. If (x mod 2 = 0) AND ALSO (x < 100) then write(x);

107. Using 'AND' in a statement suggests that there are at least ----- condition(s).

a. 4

b. 3

c. 2

d. 1

MULTI-CONDITIONAL IF STATEMENTS (using OR)

108. **Which statement is true?**

a. **OR** must always be used in a multi-conditional statement.

b. For **OR** to be used in a statement, more than 2 conditions must be present.

c. **OR** should be used if the 2 conditions in a statement are to be met to make a decision.

d. **OR** is a logical operator.

109. **Which statement is <u>FALSE</u>?**

a. OR is used in decision making.

b. If 3 conditions are in a statement, **OR** cannot be used.

c. If the 1st of 2 conditions are true when **OR** is used, the 2nd will not be tested.

d. If one of 2 conditions used with an **OR** test yields a positive result, the whole test is declared positive.

110. **Where does the major difference between OR and AND lie?**

a. In the type of statements with which they are associated.

b. The speed with which they are executed.

c. The number of conditions that must be returned positive for the entire test to be positive.

d. The position in which they appear, if used together, in a statement.

111. **A value must satisfy 1 of 2 stated criteria. What is required for the conditions?**

a. AND

b. OR

c. AND then IF

d. OR then IF

112.   **A value may satisfy either of 2 criteria. Which statement is correct?**

a.   If (x>10) OR (x div3 =1)

b.   If (x>10) AND (x div3 =1

c.   If (x>10) AND IF (x div3 =1

d.   If (x>10) OR IF (x div3 =1

NEGATING VALUES AND CONDITIONS (using NOT)

113.   **Which statement is true?**

a.   **NOT** cannot be used if there is one condition, only, in a statement.

b.   **NOT** must be used with integers, only.

c.   Statements that contain **NOT** cannot facilitate **OR** or **AND**.

d.   **NOT** reverses or negates the true value of a condition.

114.   **What does the expression, *'NOT (=)'* return?**

a.   >

b.   <

c.   <>

d.   =

115.   **What does the expression, *'NOT (<>)'* return?**

a.   =

b.   <>

c.   <

d.   >

116. Not (not(<>)) returns ----------

   a. =

   b. >=

   c. <=

   d. <>

117. Which statement is <u>FALSE</u>?

   a. NOT (false) = true

   b. NOT (true) = NOT (false)

   c. NOT (true) = fa**lse**

   d. NOT(false) = NOT(fa**lse)**

118. Which statement is true?

   a. NOT(NOT(true)) = true

   b. NOT (NOT(false)) = NOT (false)

   c. NOT (true) = NOT(NOT(true))

   d. NOT(false) = NOT(true)

USING BLOCKS OF STATEMENT WITH IF

119. What is the most logical statement re blocks of statements relating to IF?

   a. They function like paragraphs in an essay.

   b. They are units of code that carry out specific actions based upon decision statements.

   c. Their main function is to make the code easier to understand

   d. They are executed when conditions are true, only.

120.   **What is the usual feature of blocks of statements?**

a.   There are 3 or more statements.

b.   They are always in the variable declaration section of the program.

c.   They collectively perform a single task.

d.   They are enclosed by the **begin** and **end** statements.

121.   **Which statement is true?**

a.   Every block of statements must be associated with an IF statement.

b.   The last statement in a block does not require an end-of-statement punctuation mark.

c.   Statements in a block use commas at the end.

d.   There is a limit to the number of blocks that are allowed in a program.

122.   **Which statement is <u>FALSE</u>?**

a.   Some Pascal programs do not have any statement blocks.

b.   Statement blocks are not associated with identifiers.

c.   At least 1 statement block is in every Pascal program.

d.   Inner statement blocks help to make programs look structured.

123.   **Which code segment correctly establishes a block of statements?**

a. If x=2	b. If x=2	c. If x=2	d. If x=2
Y=4;	Y=4;	Begin	Begin
Z=y	Z=y;	Y=4;	Y=4;
End;		Z=y	Z=y;
		End;	

Using constants

124. **Which statement about constants is true?**

a. They are used to represent integer values, only.

b. They do not have to be declared in the program.

c. They are values that remain unchanged during the execution of a program.

d. They are values that may be changed within the program.

125. **Which keyword is used in declaring a constant?**

a. Con

b. Cont

c. Co

d. Const

126. **What is one major benefit of using constants?**

a. They allow the naming of values.

b. They allow easier editing to the code when values are to be changed.

c. Prevent confusion in using both variables and constants.

d. Sometimes less coding is required.

127. **Which is NOT a rule governing constants?**

a. They must be declared before variables are declared.

b. They must not be used in arithmetic operations.

c. They must be used with the assignment operator.

d. They must be identified by valid identifiers.

128. A program is to do routine calculations that convert students' scores to percentages and add and average these. Which statement is best for efficient programming?

a. Scores should be variables,   the 'hundred' representing percent, a constant

b. Scores should be constant,   the 'hundred' representing percent, a variable

c. Scores should be variables,   the 'hundred' representing percent, a variable

d. Scores should be constants,   the 'hundred' representing percent, a constant

129. Which constant declaration is correct?

a. Cons miles = 10;

b. Con days = 5;

c. Const ID = P095'

d. Const Size = 10;

THE FOR LOOP

130. Which statement about the *for* loop is true?

a. It is a pre-condition loop.

b. It must work with blocks of more than 3 statements.

c. It cannot accommodate the **if** statement.

d. The controlling condition of the loop is at the end.

131. Which statement about the for loop is FALSE?

a. Its initial statement sets up the number of cycles to be executed.

b. It is referred to as a post-condition loop.

c. One **for loop** may be set up in another.

d. It is a finite loop – it runs for a set number of cycles.

132. How many cycles will be executed by the following? For c:= 2 to 5 do

    a. 5

    b. 4

    c. 3

    d. 2

133. How many cycles will be executed by the following? For i:= 0 to 2 do

    a. 5

    b. 4

    c. 3

    d. 2

134. What will be the value of x after the loop is completed?

x=1

For i:= 1 to 4 do

  Begin

    x:= x+i

  End;

    a. 3

    b. 4

    c. 5

    d. 6

THE WHILE LOOP

135.   **Which statement about the while loop is true?**

    a. It is a pre-condition loop.

    b. It is a post-condition loop.

    c. It is a finite loop.

    d. It uses less code than the **for** loop.

136.   **Which statement about the while loop is false?**

    a. It is an infinite loop.

    b. It can contain a for loop.

    c. It gives more flexibility than the for loop.

    d. It needs to work with some previously initialized value.

137.   **What should be output from the following?**

```
x=1;

While x < 3 do

 Begin

   Write(x);

   x:=x +1

 end;
```

    a. 1,2,3

    b. 1,2

    c. 2,1

    d. 3,2,1

138.   **What will be output by the following?**

x=0;

While x< 4 do

Begin

Write('');*

x:=x +1

end;

a. * *

b. * * *

c. * * * *

d. * * * * *

139.   **A routine is to be written to accept 5 values. Which of the following is correct?**

a. *n=1;*

while n < 5 do

begin

read(m);

n:= n+ 1

end;

b. *n:=0;*

while n < 5 do

begin

read(m);

n:=n+1

end;

c. *n:=10;*

while n <= 15 do

begin

read(m);

n:=n+1

end;

d. *n:=5;*

while n < 9 do

begin

read(m);

n:=n+1

end;

TERMINATORS

140. **What is a terminator?**

a. A value

b. An operation

c. An expression

d. A very short routine

141. **What is the purpose of a terminator?**

a. To feed values to the while loop.

b. To join conditions in the while loop.

c. To indicate the end of a data input stream.

d. To initialize a constant in the while loop.

142. **Which term is <u>NOT</u> used to refer to a terminator?**

a. Dummy value

b. Rogue value

c. Sentinel value

d. End value

143. **Which statement about a terminator is true?**

a. It must be an integer

b. It must be a real value

c. It may be a char or string

d. It may be integer, real, string or char

144.   **Which is a guideline for using a terminator?**

a. One should know the number of data items for input.

b. The input must be arranged in some given order.

c. The terminator must be of the same type of the input data but must **not** be within the data range.

d. The terminator must be of the same type of the input data but must be within the data range.

USING A TERMINATOR WITH THE WHILE LOOP

145.   **A program is to accept student scores [0-100]. Which of the following is a valid terminator?**

a. 100

b. 0

c. 50

d. -99

146.   **A program is to accept integers, 0-50. Which is the best value to use for a terminator?**

a. 51

b. -999

c. -1

d. 100

147.   **A program is to accept single alphabetic characters for processing. Which is valid terminator?**

a. 'x'

b. '9'

c. X

d. 9

148. **Which statement is <u>NOT</u> true?**

a. A terminator is not a part of the condition in a **while** loop.

b. A terminator is a part of the condition in a **while** loop.

c. A read statement outside of the loop passes the terminator to the loop.

d. The terminator is the same data type as the data with which it is associated.

149. **In which statement is the terminator correctly used?**

a. While -999 = mark do

b. While mark < -999 do

c. While mark <> -999 do

d. While mark > -999 do

THE REPEAT LOOP

150. **Which statement about the repeat loop is true?**

a. It is similar to the while loop.

b. It is a pre-condition loop.

c. **Begin** and **end** must be used to group statements in the loop.

d. All statements between **repeat** and **until** are treated as a block.

151. **Which statement about the repeat loop is true?**

a. The condition is at the end.

b. It uses multi-conditions, only.

c. It has the same ending as the **while** loop.

d. It always uses less code than the **for** loop.

152.   **In which situation should a repeat loop be used instead of a for loop?**

a.   100 values make up the input stream.

b.   5 letters of the alphabet make up the input stream.

c.   A defined number of data items are to be read from a file.

d.   An undefined number of scores are to be processed.

153.   **In which situation should a repeat loop be used instead of a while loop?**

a.   There are at least 10 items in the input stream.

b.   There are more than 20 items in the input stream.

c.   There is uncertainty of any item being in the input stream

d.   A suitable terminator has been identified.

154.   **How many marks will be read, according to the following?**

x:=1;

repeat

  read(mark);

  x:=x+1

until x: = 5;

a.   5

b.   4

c.   3

d.   2

IF-THEN-ELSE VS CASE

155.   What is <u>NOT</u> an advantage of using the case statement over the if-then-else statement?

a.   The program will be correct.

b.   It makes the code easier to read.

c.   **The** logic of the program is easier followed.

d.   Testing will be easier facilitated.

156.   In which situation would it be a clear advantage to use a case statement instead of an if-then-else statement?

a.   Students' scores are to be input and classified, A-F.

b.   Scores are to be input to determine pass or failure.

c.   Two unequal values are to be input to determine the higher and lower.

d.   To determine and output the gender of applicants.

157.   Which statement is <u>NOT</u> true?

a.   If-then-else and case statements can accomplish the same tasks.

b.   If-then-else and case statements may both be multi-conditional statements.

c.   If-then-else and case statements have the same structure.

d.   If-then-else and case statements have different structures.

158.   **What is the case equivalence of the following?**

*If unit_price >= 1000 then discount := unit _price * .1*

*else If unit_price >= 850 then discount := unit _price * .15*

*else If unit_price >= 500 then discount := unit _price * .2*

else discount := 0;

a. *case **unit_price** of*

   *1000..9999 : discount:=unit_price * 10/100;*

   *850..999 : discount:=unit_price * 15/100;*

   *500..849 : discount:=unit_price * 20/100;*

    else discount :=0;

  end;

b. *case **unit_price** of*

   *< 1000..9999 : discount:=unit_price * 10/100;*

   *< 850..999 : discount:=unit_price * 15/100;*

   *< 500..849 : discount:=unit_price * 20/100;*

    else discount :=0;

  end;

c. *case **unit_price** of*

   *> 1000 : discount:=unit_price * 10/100;*

   *>850: discount:=unit_price * 15/100;*

   *>500: discount:=unit_price * 20/100;*

    else discount :=0;

  end;

d. *case **unit_price** of*

   >1000..9999 :
*discount:=unit_price * 10/100;*

   > 850..999 :
*discount:=unit_price * 15/100;*

   >500..849 :
*discount:=unit_price * 20/100;*

    > else discount :=0;

  end;

159. **What is the if-then-else equivalence of the following?**

```
case score of
        80..100 : grade:='A';
        60..79 : grade:= 'B';
        50..69 : grade:='C';
        else grade:='F';
end;
```

a. If score <> 80 then grade := 'A'
        else If score <> 60 then grade:= 'B'
            else If score <> 50 then grade := 'C'
                else grade := 'F';

b. If score = 80 then grade := 'A'
        else If score = 60 then grade:= 'B'
            else If score = 50 then grade := 'C'
                else grade := 'F';

c. If score >= 80 then grade := 'A'
        else If score >= 60 then grade:= 'B'
            else If score >= 50 then grade := 'C'
                else grade := 'F';

d. If score <= 80 then grade := 'A'
        else If score <= 60 then grade:= 'B'
            else If score <= 50 then grade := 'C'
                else grade := 'F';

ARRAYS

160.   **Which statement about arrays is true?**

a.   Arrays are data structures which store collections of data items (of the same type) in consecutive memory locations in RAM.

b.   Arrays are data structures which store collections of data items (of the same type) in no given order in RAM.

c.   Arrays are storage structures that store integers, only.

d.   Arrays are storage structures that store strings, only.

161.   **Which description does <u>NOT</u> relate to arrays?**

a.   *LOCATION:* One of the designated areas for storing data items individually.

b.   *ELEMENTS OR VALUES*: The data items which are stored.

c.   *MEMORY POINTERS:* Numbers that indicate where the data items are stored in RAM.

d.   *SUBSCRIPT OR INDEX***:** A number or label that identifies a location.

162.   **What does linear or sequential access mean in relation to arrays?**

a.   To begin at one end of the array and move through the locations consecutively.

b.   To go directly to a specific location in the array.

c.   To begin at one end of the array and move through the locations consecutively or otherwise.

d.   Use random generated numbers in determining locations to visit.

163.   **What does direct access mean in relation to arrays?**

a.   To begin at one end of the array and move through the locations consecutively.

b.   To go directly to a specific location in the array.

c.   To begin at one end of the array and move through the locations consecutively or otherwise.

d.   Use random generated numbers in determining locations to visit.

164.   **To what do boundaries and size refer in relation to arrays?**

a.   The lowest and highest data values and the number of elements that may be stored.

b.   The lowest or highest subscript values and the number of elements that are stored.

c.   The lowest and highest subscript values and the number of data elements that are stored.

d.   The lowest and highest subscript values and the number of elements that may be stored.

THE TYPE STATEMENT

165.   **Why is the type statement necessary?**

a.   As an option for programmers.

b.   All programs require it.

c.   The basic Pascal data types are inadequate for some programming requirements.

d.   The basic Pascal data types are sometimes unavailable to programmers.

166.   **Which statement about the type statement is _FALSE_?**

a.   It allows the programmer to create his/her own data type.

b.   Its use suggests that all basic data types have been used in the program.

c.   It may be used to create a data type with specified values.

d.   It may be used to create a structured type of any of the basic types.

167.   **Which statement about the type statement is most logical?**

a.   It functions as a supplement to the basic data types.

b.   It is efficient to use type in all programming situations.

c.   Its use results in much shorter programs.

d.   It does not impact the readability of code.

168. **Which is a popular use of the type statement?**

a. Initialize integer values

b. Set up customized array structures

c. Reserve storage space for string values

d. Initialize char values

169. **Which task may be accomplished by the type statement, only?**

a. Overwrite integer values with real values

b. Convert integer values to string values

c. Declare 5 successive integers on one line

d. Set up a uniquely structured type.

DECLARING ARRAYS

170. **What does '1..8' indicate in the statement, *Type Scores_Array_Type = ARRAY [1..8] of integer; ?***

a. The number of elements in the array.

b. The size of the array.

c. The lower and upper boundaries or range of the array.

d. The data elements of the arrays

171. **What is the name of the array as indicated in the statement, Type Scores_Array_Type = ARRAY [1..8] of integer; ?**

a. ARRAY

b. Scores_Array_Type

c. Of Integer

d. Not included

172.   **State the purpose of Type in: *Type Scores_Array_Type = ARRAY [1..8] of integer;***

a.   It sets up an array profile, with a profile name and profile structure.

b.   It sets up an array of integer values.

c.   It defines the range, only, of the array.

d.   It indicates how many values will be read into the array.

173.   **How useful is the approach in declaring arrays using *Type*?**

a.   It prevents out-of-range array errors.

b.   It requires less programming effort than other methods.

c.   It allows arrays with the same structure to be declared by just using **var**.

d.   It allows faster access to the array.

Type Marks = ARRAY [1..40] of real; Based on the preceding, which statement would declare an array, Form2, to hold the same number and type of data elements?

a.   Type : Form2

b.   Var Form2: Marks;

c.   Var Marks: Form2;

d.   Type: Form2;

LOADING AN ARRAY DIRECTLY BY ASSIGNMENT

174.   ***ScoresArray[1];* What does the preceding statement indicate?**

a.   There is an array with the value '1'.

b.   The 2nd position in 'ScoresArray' is referenced.

c.   The array can hold 1 value, only.

d.   One integer is to be input into an array.

175.   **Given the statement, *ScoresArray[2]; how many elements can the array hold?***

   a. Not indicated

   b. No more than 2

   c. 3

   d. 2

176.   **Given the statement, *ScoresArray[2]:=1; what is indicated?***

   a. '1' is placed in the 3rd location of the array.

   b. '1' is placed in the 2nd location of the array.

   c. '1' is placed in any location in the array.

   d. 1 element should be placed into the array

177.   **Given the statement, *ScoresArray[2]:=1; what is the purpose of '[ ]'?***

   a. To indicate that the array has values

   b. To indicate that the array is functional

   c. To enclose the values which operate as references for the locations/positions

   d. To enclose the values which are to be assigned to the locations/positions

178.   **Given the statements, *ScoresArray[0]:=1; ScoresArray[1]:=2;* which values are assigned to the array?**

   a. 1,0

   b. 1,2

   c. 1,1

   d. 02

LOADING AN ARRAY DIRECTLY FROM KEYBOARD INPUT

179. **What is accomplished by the following statement?** *Read(ScoreArray[1]);*

   a. A value is loaded into the array after being entered at the keyboard.

   b. The value, '1' is assigned to the array within the program.

   c. A value is assigned to the 1st position of the array.

   d. The array is initialized for loading.

180. **What is accomplished by the following statements?** *Read (x); ScoreArray[1]:= x;*

   a.   x is loaded directly into the array from the keyboard.

   b. x is generated in the program and loaded into the array.

   c. x is read at the keyboard and loaded directly into the array.

   d. x is read at the keyboard then assigned to the array.

181. **Which is the best description for the fo**llowing operation? *ScoreArray[0]:=1;*

   a. Indirect access

   b. Sequential access

   c. Direct access

   d. indexed access

LOADING AN ARRAY SEQUENTIALY FROM KEYBOARD INPUT

182. **What is the purpose of 'c' in the following?**

   For c := 0 to 2 do

   Read(LettersArray[c]),

   a. To open the array for direct loading.

   b. To reference the locations within the array.

   c. To assign 0 directly to the array.

   d. To accept the array values from the keyboard.

183. How many values/elements should be loaded into the array by the following?

For c := 0 to 2 do

Read(LettersArray[c]),

a. 0

b. 1

c. 2

d. 3

184. Which mode of array access best describes the following?

For i := 1 to 5 do

Read(LettersArray[i]),

a. Indexed

b. Random

c. Sequential

d. Direct

185. Which error would result if an array is declared to hold 5 elements and the following statements are executed?

For i := 0 to 5 do

Read(LettersArray[i]),

a. Data type

b. sequential

c. initialization

d. out-of-range

186.   Which values would be loaded into array, Scores, with the following statements?

For i := 0 to 3 do

Scores[i]:= i+1;

a. 1,2,3,4

b. 0,1,2,3

c. 1,2,3

d. 0,1,2

ADDING VALUES TO AN ARRAY

187.   **Four input** values **(2,4,3,5)** are represented by 'n'. **What would** be the total immediately after the 3rd input value as indicated by the following statements?

total := 0;

For c := 1 to 4 do

begin

Read(n);

total := total + n

End;

a. 7

b. 9

c. 12

d. 13

LINEAR OR SEQUENTIAL SEARCH OF ARRAY

188.   **For the fo**llowing program segment to be effective, 'found' would have to be declared as a ………. data type.

Repeat

If SearchValue = ScoresArray[counter] then Found = True;

Counter := counter + 1;

Until (Found = true) OR (Counter > 3);

If found = true then write('Value found') else write('Value not found');

End;

a. Boolean

b. Integer

c. Real

d. Char

189.   **What is an advantage for using a repeat loop over a for loop when searching for a data item in an array?**

a.   If the element being sought is absent, there will not be a programming error.

b.   The repeat loop is much easier to use.

c.   If the element being sought is the 1st in the array, the search will take less time.

d.   Errors may be prevented during the search.

190.   **Which statement is true re performance of the repeat and for loops?**

a.   If the element being sought is the last in the list, there is no difference in performance.

b.   If the element being sought is in the middle of the list, there is no difference in performance.

c.   If the element being sought is not in the list, there is a difference in performance.

d.   If the element being sought is repeated in the list, there is no difference in performance between the **repeat** and **for** loops.

USING THE 'STRING' DATA TYPE

191. Which statement about any string data value is true?

a. It is equivalent to an array of characters.

b. It is equivalent to an array of integers.

c. It is regarded as being among basic data types.

d. It cannot be used in the same program with char.

192. Which statement about strings is <u>NOT</u> true?

a. They may be declared like normal variables.

b. Digits may make up parts of strings.

c. Digits must not make up parts of strings.

d. They may be used in read statements like normal variables.

193. Which is <u>NOT</u> a correct declaration of a string?

a. Var grade : string;

b. Var grade: string[4];

c. Var grade: string [x];

d. Var grade; string:

194. Which input value could be most suitably used for a string?

a. Someone's age

b. Someone's score on a test

c. The size of someone's shoes

d. Someone's address.

COMPARING CHARACTERS AND STRINGS

195. **Which statement about characters is true?**

    a. Characters are ordinal values because they are ordered elements within a series.

    b. Characters are not members of the ASCII set.

    c. Characters cannot be compared in the way that numbers are compared.

    d. Digits cannot be used as characters.

196. **Which statement about char or string is <u>NOT</u> true?**

    a. String contains members of the ASCII set.

    b. One char may be greater than another.

    c. A digit may be used as a char.

    d. A string cannot be compared with another.

197. **Which statement is <u>NOT</u> true?**

    a. A string may be a super set of a character.

    b. A character may be a sub set of a string.

    c. A digit cannot be the first element of a string.

    d. A string should occupy more storage space than a character.

    e.

PROGRAM COMMENTS

198. **Which statement about comments is true?**

    a. They signal the end of programs to the compiler.

    b. They signal the start of the program to the compiler.

    c. They cause the program to execute faster.

    d. They are helpful in explaining how the program works.

199. **Which statement about comments is <u>NOT</u> true?**

a. They are inserted into programs by enclosing them within pairs of braces, {}.

b. They are normally long sentences and cause the programs to work slower.

c. They are useful especially for programmers in carrying out program maintenance.

d. They are ignored by the compiler and may be inserted anywhere in the program.

200. **What is the main reason for using comments in a program?**

a. To indicate to the compiler how the program should work.

b. To make the program readable and understandable by humans.

c. To indicate to humans the number of lines in the program.

d. To create external description and documentation for the program.

201. **Which statement is <u>NOT</u> true?**

a. Comments may be referred to as internal program documentation.

b. It is possible to have unnecessary or redundant comments.

c. The use of meaningful identifiers will help to keep comments at a minimal level.

d. A comment must not appear before the first executable statement of a program.

202. **How many comments are in the following code segment?**

n1 := 1.0; {The value of 1.0 is assigned to the first variable}

n2 := 2.5;

n3 := n1 + n2; {The values of the variables are added, and the result assigned to

a third variable}

writeln('sum is ',n3:4:2); {The result is displayed using 4 character spaces and 2

decimal places}

a. 4   b. 3   c. 2   d. 1

STANDARD FUNCTIONS

203.   Which statement about standard functions is true?

   a.   The program must use complex code to create them.

   b.   They are available to the programmer within the compiler.

   c.   They may be used with arithmetic operations, only.

   d.   They must be declared before they are used.

204.   Which set has 2 standard functions?

   a.   ABS, ODD

   b.   ABS, WRITE

   c.   WRITE, SQRT

   d.   SQRT, READ

205.   What is the purpose of the TRUNC function?

   a.   Returns the decimal part of a real number.

   b.   Returns the whole part of an integer.

   c.   Returns the decimal part of a real number.

   d.   Separates the whole and decimal parts of a real number.

206.   **What is returned by the application of the following functions?** *ODD (31), ROUND(4.4)*

   a.   true, 0.4

   b.   false, 4

   c.   true, 4

   d.   false, 0.4

207.   The SQRT function returns the root of a number in ---------------format.

    a.   Integer

    b.   Boolean

    c.   Char

    d.   Real

208.   What will SQRT(4) return?

    a.   2.0000000000E+00

    b.   2.0000000000+00

    c.   2.0

    d.   2

209.   Which of the functions is not a standard mathematical function?

    a.   SQR

    b.   LENGTH

    c.   ABS

    d.   ODD

210.   Which set has 2 string functions?

    a.   TRUNC, CONCAT

    b.   CONCAT, SQR

    c.   ROUND, ABS

    d.   COPY, INSERT

211.   The COPY function returns a/the ---------- of a string.

    a.   subset

    b.   beginning

    c.   ending

    d.   substring

212.   **The INSERT function places a ---------- into a string.**

a. Substring

b. Integer

c. Comment

d. variable

APPLICATION OF STRING FUNCTIONS

213.   **What is the output from the following Program?**

```
Program ConcatFunction;

uses wincrt;

var

 S,T,U: String;

 begin

   T := 'PAS';

   U := 'CAL';

   S := Concat(T,U);

   writeln(S)

end.
```

a. PAS

b. CAL

c. TU

d. PASCAL

214.   What is the output from the following program?

```
Program InsertFunction;

uses wincrt;

var

  S: String;

begin

  S := 'Honesty is the policy.';

  Insert('best ', S, 16);

  write (S)

end.
```

a.   Honesty is the best

b.   Honesty is the policy.

c.   Honesty is best.

d.   None of the above.

215.   What is the output from the following program?

```
Program CopyFunction;

uses wincrt;

var S: String;

begin

  S := 'PASCAL';

  S := Copy( S, 2, 3);

  writeln(s)

end.
```

a.   CAS   b.   ASC   c.   PAS   d.   CAL

216. **What is the output from the following program?**

Program DeleteFunction;

uses wincrt;

var

S: string;

begin

S := 'You should not be Honest.';

Delete(s,12,3);

writeln(S);

end.

a. Be Honest

b. Should be Honest

c. You should be Honest

d. None of the above

MODULAR PROGRAMMING

217. **Which is <u>NOT</u> a true statement re modular programming?**

a. It is a 'divide-and-conquer' approach to programming.

b. The program is developed in manageable sections (modules) then integrated.

c. The use of standard functions is compulsory.

d. It is normally used for large programs.

218. **In modular programming, what is true when the top-down approach is used?**

a. The details are worked out first then integrated to form a general picture.

b. The general idea is dealt with first, followed by various levels of details.

c. The details are organized then structured into modules.

d. Modules are first created then the levels of details worked out.

219.   In modular programming, what is true when the bottom-up approach is used?

a. The general idea is dealt with first, followed by various levels of details.

b. The details are organized then structured into modules.

c. The details are worked out first then integrated to form a general picture.

d. Modules are first created then the levels of details worked out.

220.   In Pascal, modular programming is facilitated by -------------- procedures and functions.

a. Compiler-generated

b. Programmer-defined

c. Standard mathematical

d. Standard string

221.   In modular programming, each module should perform ---------- task(s), only.

a. 4

b. 3

c. 2

d. 1

222.   Which task is not expected to be performed by a module?

a. displaying an option menu

b. calculating average marks

c. declaring string variables

d. searching an array

223.   **Which statement is NOT true?**

a.   A procedure bears the features and format of a normal program.

b.   A module, like a program, can have a period (.) following the **end** statement.

c.   A module is known by its name and consists of a set of program statements.

d.   The statements in a module are grouped using the **begin** and **end** keywords.

224.   **What is the basic format of a Pascal modular program, paying attention to sequence?**

a.   Data declaration, header , procedures, main part of program

b.   Header, main part of program, procedures, data declaration

c.   Header, data declaration, procedures, main part of program

d.   Header, main part of program, data declaration, procedures

225.   What are the names of the procedures in the following code?

```
procedure display_title;

begin

    writeln('This program calculates the total pay for an employee') ;

    writeln(' based on hours worked and the hourly rate of pay.')

end;

procedure get_data;

begin

    writeln('Please enter the number of  hours. Eg. 10'');

    readln( hours);

    writeln('Please enter the hourly rate');

    readln( rate)

end;
```

procedure calculate_pay;

begin

*pay:= hours * rate*

end;

procedure display_pay;

begin

writeln('The total pay is \$', pay:4:2,)'

end;

a. Procedure display_title, procedure get_data

b. Procedure calculate_pay, procedure get_data, procedure display pay, procedure display_title

c. display_title, calculate pay,

d. calculate_pay, get_data, display_ pay,display_title

226.   Which is the correct header and data declaration for the procedures in question 226?

a.   Program Using_Procedures;

uses wincrt;

var   hours, rate, pay : real;

b.   Using_Procedures;

uses wincrt;

var   hours, rate, pay : real;

c.   Program Using_Procedures;

uses wincrt;

Const   hours, rate, pay : real;

d.   Program Using_Procedures;

Uses wincrt;

var   hours, rate, pay : integer;

227. **Which is the correct program segment for activating the procedures in question 226?**

a. *begin*

   get_data

   calculate_pay;

   display_pay

  end.

b. *begin*

   display_title;

   get_data

   display_pay

  end.

c. *begin*

   display_title;

   get_data ;

   calculate_pay;

   display_pay

  end;

d. *begin*

   get_data

   calculate_pay;

   display_pay

  end.

ARITHMETIC OPERATOR PRECEDENCE

228.   Pascal has certain pre-defined rules that are followed in arithmetic, thus giving priority to the various operators. What is the correct priority of the operators from highest to lowest?

a. *,   /, mod,   div,   +,   -

b. *,   mod,   /,   div,   +,   -

c. *,   /,   div,   mod,   +,   -

d. /,   *,   mod,   div,   +,   -

The operators are always evaluated left to right, but parentheses may be used to override the order of precedence. QUESTIONS 230 – 236 are based on the following program.

```
Program OperatorPrecedence;

uses wincrt;

var num1,num2,num3 : integer;  result : real;

begin

 num1 := 1;    num2 := 2;    num3 := 4;

 result1 := num1 + num2 / num3; writeln(resul1t:4:2);   [0.13]

 result2 := num1 * num2 * num3; writeln(result2:4:2);   [1.50]

 result3 := num1 * num2 - num3; writeln(result3:4:2);   [8.00]

 result4:= num1 + num2 + num3; writeln(result4:4:2);  [-2.00]

 result5 := num1 / num2 * num3; writeln(result5:4:2);   [7.00]

 result6 := num1 * num2 / num3; writeln(result6:4:2);   [2.00]

 result7 := num1 + num2 - num3; writeln(result7:4:2);   [-1.00]

End.
```

What are the output values for the variables, result1 –result7?

229.   Result1

    a. 1.30

    b. 1.03

    c. 0.13

    d. 0.10

234.   Result5

    a. 6.00

    b. 6.44

    c. 6.83

    d. 7.00

230.   Result2

    a. 0.15

    b. 1.00

    c. 1.15

    d. 1.50

235.   Result6

    a. 1.15

    b. 19

    c. 2.00

    d. 2.50

231.   Result3

    a. 8.00

    b. 8.05

    c. 8.10

    d. 8.50

236. Result7

    a. -0.95

    b. -1.00

    c. -1.45

    d. -1.50

232.   Result4

    a. 2.00

    b. 1.50

    c. -1.50

    d. -2.00

ANSWERS

1. b	51. b	25. b	73. a	97. a
2. d	52. c	26. c	74. c	98. a
3. b	53. b	27. a	75. b	99. d
4. d	54. b	28. c	76. a	100. d
5. a	55. a	29. d	77. d	101. a
6. b	56. d	30. d	78. a	102. c
7. a	57. b	31. b	79. c	103. c
8. d	58. d	32. b	80. c	104. a
9. c	59. a	33. d	81. d	105. c
10. a	60. c	34. c	82. c	106. a
11. b	61. b	35. d	83. a	107. c
12. b	62. d	36. b	84. c	108. d
13. d	63. a	37. b	85. b	109. d
14. c	64. d	38. d	86. d	110. c
15. a	65. a	39. a	87. c	111. b
16. c	66. c	40. b	88. b	112. a
17. b	67. d	41. c	89. a	113. d
18. c	68. c	42. b	90. a	114. c
19. d	69. b	43. d	91. a	115. a
20. b	70. a	44. c	92. c	116. d
21. d	71. c	45. c	93. a	117. b
22. a	72. c	46. a	94. a	118. a
23. a	73. d	47. c	95. b	119. b
24. c	74. c	48. b	96. c	120. d

121. b	145. d	169. d	193. c	217. c
122. a	146. b	170. c	194. d	218. c
123. c	147. d	171. d	195. d	219. b
124. c	148. a	172. a	196. a	220. c
125. d	149. c	173. c	197. d	221. b
126. b	150. d	174. b	198. c	222. d
127. b	151. a	175. b	199. d	223. c
128. a	152. d	176. a	200. b	224. b
129. d	153. c	177. a	201. b	225. c
130. a	154. c	178. c	202. d	226. d
131. b	155. a	179. b	203. b	227. a
132. b	156. a	180. d	204. b	228. c
133. c	157. c	181. d	205. a	229. c
134. c	158. a	182. c	206. b.	230. c
135. a	159. c	183. c	207. c	231. d
136. d	160. a	184. d	208. d	232. a
137. c	161. c	185. c	209. a	233. d
138. c	162. a	186. d	210. b	234. d
139. b	163. b	187. a	211. d	235. c
140. a	164. d	188. b	212. d	236. b
141. c	165. c	189. a	213. a	
142. d	166. b	190. c	214. d	
143. d	167. a	191. a.	215. d	
144. c	168. b	192. a	216. b	

www.ingramcontent.com/pod-product-compliance
Lightning Source LLC
Chambersburg PA
CBHW080850250726

48663CB00003B/405